Introduction

THE IDEA OF DWELLING is used all over the Bible. Sometimes it means to live together. Sometimes it means to sit. Sometimes, it means to wait.

People who live or sit or wait together often get to know each other pretty well. And a good thing about that is, after a time, we may be more likely to understand each other, more likely to consult each other. We become part of each other's imagination.

In much the same way, Dwelling in the Word of God as a ritual part of shared life enriches the imagination of many kinds of groups.

For years, we have read Luke 10: 1-12 as we dwell in the Word. These verses are as integral to our staff meeting as the coffee. In a two-hour meeting we spend at least 30 minutes dwelling, seeing how this living Word, from the God whose children we are, might speak to us that day.

Assemblies of Hundreds of People

Dwelling in the Word can be used in groups small and large. We have watched dwelling take place in every size of group, from Partnership for Missional Church clusters to consultant training to assembly and convention work with hundreds of people. We hope after reading this little book that your group will dwell in the Word together, too.

Dwelling in the Word

A POCKET HANDBOOK

PAT TAYLOR ELLISON
PATRICK KEIFERT

CHURCH
INNOVATIONS

Dwelling in the Word
Copyright © 2011 Pat Taylor Ellison and Patrick Keifert.

Published in St Paul, Minnesota by
Church Innovations Institute, Incorporated
1563 Como Avenue #103
St Paul, Mn 55108
www.churchinnovations.org

First edition 2011
Cover & interior design: Lookout Design, Inc.
(www.lookoutdesign.com)

ISBN 10:   0-9829313-1-X
ISBN 13: 978-0-9829313-1-8
Printed in the United States of America

18 17 16 15 14 13 12 11   1 2 3 4 5 6 7 8

Table of Contents

Chapter 1

FIRST, JUST DO IT.

HERE ARE THE STEPS for Dwelling in the Word:

1. Start with a prayer, inviting the Spirit to guide your attending to the Word of God.

2. Turn to Luke 10:1-12. Later you may choose your own passage, a story related to the story of your group's work. But start with Luke 10: 1-12, because it works for many people all over the world—it is a good starting place. Have Bibles or copies of the passage available. Set aside without apology at least 20 minutes for this activity.

3. Begin with one person reading this passage aloud to the group. Then allow some silence to unfold as people let the words have their impact.

4. Next, instruct folks in this way:

   Find a person in the group you know least well (we call this person a "reasonably friendly-looking stranger"). Listen that person into free speech as he or she tells you what they heard in the passage.

   Listen that person into answering one of two questions: 1.) What captured your imagination? or 2.) What question would you like to ask a Biblical scholar? Listen well, because your job will be to report to the rest of the group what your partner has said, not what you yourself said. Note-taking is OK.

5. Then, turn folks loose with their partners for 6-10 minutes. Notice how they pay attention to one another. When you draw them back together, ask for them to tell what they learned from their partners.

6. Then, wrestle together as a group. Ask, "What might God might be up to in the passage for us today?"

   Let people know that, as your conversation on other matters continues, anyone at any time may call for the Gospel, and the group will return to the passage once again.

LUKE 10: 1-12

After
this   the
Lord   appointed
seventy others and sent
them on ahead of him in pairs to
every town and place where he himself
intended to go. He said to them, "The harvest
is plentiful, but the laborers are few; therefore ask the
Lord of the harvest to send out laborers into his harvest. Go
on your way. See, I am sending you out like lambs into the
midst of wolves. Carry no purse, no bag, no sandals; and
greet no one on the road. Whatever house you enter, first
say, 'Peace to this house!' And if anyone is there who shares
in peace your peace will rest on that person; but if not, it
will return to you. Remain in the same house, eating and
drinking whatever they provide, for the laborer deserves to
be paid. Do not move about from house to house. Whenever
you enter a town and its people welcome you, eat what is
set before you; cure the sick who are there, and say to them,
'The kingdom of God has come near to you.' But whenever
you enter a town and they   do not welcome you,
go out into its streets   and say, 'Even the
dust of your town that   clings to our feet,
we wipe off in protest   against you. Yet
know this: the kingdom   of God has come
near.' I tell you, on that   day it will be more
tolerable   for   Sodom   than for that town.
(NRSV)

The Word in Which We Dwell.

CHURCH INNOVATIONS INSTITUTE

Chapter 2

WHAT HAPPENS?

SIMPLE INSTRUCTIONS. Simple process. Right?

Here are three brief tales of what comes of Dwelling in the Word.

TALE #1

Picture leaders from a dozen or more congregations meeting for the first time in Port Elizabeth, South Africa. They are from different denominations and cultures and classes, some of which were explicitly created by the rules of apartheid that divided culture and race, even in the same denomination. They have not really met with one another in a joint project before now. And they bring very different worship patterns and traditions.

The local leader invites them to worship together as their first joint act. They are already anxious, and the simple fact that they share almost no ritual worship practices or music intensifies their anxiety. The body language is clear and painful. The congregations are further apart, even literally, at the end of the worship service than they were at the start. Almost everyone has experienced significant embarrassment or shame during parts of the worship.

Now imagine all of them being asked to 1) listen to the Luke 10 text as it is read and then 2) find that reasonably friendly-looking stranger. Strangers are plentiful. But then add the fact that the facilitator insists that the stranger be from across denominational lines. This seems to be a recipe for disaster. First, no movement. And silence. Then, a few folks cross the floor and cross the massive gaps between the congregations, finding a reasonably friendly-looking stranger. It almost looks like a junior high school dance. Some stand with their hands in their pockets or behind their backs, giving no one eye contact; others simply avoid the task and turn to a fellow congregation member beside them. The facilitator quietly reminds them to cross the boundaries. Finally, most make the perilous journey and cross the boundaries. The opening moments look painful. Nervous smiles and laughter, quiet control, and open discomfort are everywhere. Then the miracle happens.

Respectful Conversations
Across Cultures

First one, and then another, begins to listen, really listen, and they lean into what they are hearing. Then something even more amazing happens: people start feeling heard by someone from across a boundary. They will later report that they had never in their lives been heard across that boundary on something so near and dear to them as the Word of God. Yet in one more way the simple truth is revealed that the Church is, by the will of the Father, in the person of the Son, and by the power of the Holy Spirit, a creature of the Word of God.

Deep Listening to Each Other

They dared to listen deeply to one another and notice things. Such deep listening is rare enough in group meetings. Even rarer is having to report to the rest of the

Listening for God's Word both makes clear and puts in their proper places the differ- ences between them

group what the *other* person said in a way that honors the other and ensures their safety to say freely what needs to be said. Wouldn't it be freeing to be in such a setting? Wouldn't it build trust? Wouldn't it make that group co-creators

with God of a trustworthy world?

TALE #2

Picture a major metropolitan church that has had three different senior ministers in five years. Imagine the pain in the leadership who had met each senior pastor with such great hopes and expectations.

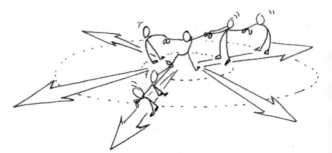

A Congregation Being Pulled Apart

With each disappointing ending of a pastor's leadership these leaders' hope diminishes and their grief increases, as does their anxiety. Old conflicts have intensified, and the leaders are ready to fight or flee. Differences they might once have lived with now seem church-dividing.

But picture a key lay leader inviting them to dwell in the same Word over a significant period of time. Instead of doing Bible studies that apply texts to the subjects of the controversies that divide them, they begin to form a shared sense of the challenge facing them. The challenge that they share is much greater and more compelling than the things that divide them. More importantly, the practice of dwelling encourages them to listen for God's preferred future, not just their own preferences.

Deep Listening for God

Coming together even with great divisions, and then articulating and wrestling with a shared even deeper question, all the while expecting to hear God speak to them through the Word and through one another, they are able to distinguish and rank the importance of the matters over which they disagree. Listening for God's Word not only makes clear but also puts into their proper places the true differences between them, and it also frees the leadership to establish some order for their deciding.

While they do not pretend to be absolutely certain of God's preferred future for their church, they now stop making their differences church-dividing.

TALE #3

Picture a church governance board that is constantly frustrated with the task of recruiting inactive or less active members to do what the governing board believes needs to be done. Then picture one of their officers introducing the practice of Dwelling in the Word, and picture the council committing to remain in that passage for a season, listening to it and to one another. Imagine them, little by little, beginning to hear God calling them into a part of God's mission in their community.

Making Plans to Convince People to Do What the Council Thinks Should Happen

Searching to Discover God's Preferred Future and Inviting People to Hear God's Missional Call

Then they see that the real issue is not convincing people to do what the council thinks should happen, but instead inviting all their members to experience God's missional call.

Shaping imagination and community for Christian vocation

Really living inside a story over time begins to shape a group's collective imagination. Over and over again, in that familiar house, re-meeting those beautiful and annoying words, a sense of shared culture grows. The habit of listening so carefully to the other as to be able to report the other's words faithfully to the group, that listening habit creates community and builds trust among them.

When trust is built in a community, that community can withstand risks and entrances and exits and big change.

It's good to know that the Spirit provides everything we need to be able to adapt to big change. Our God is a God who loves the world and is in mission to it. Dwelling in the Word shapes church leaders' imaginations to seek their missional vocation.

This pocket handbook is meant to give any congregation member:

1. some minimum "how-to" knowledge for dwelling in the Word,

2. some of the attitudes and beliefs that stand under it and upon which the practice has been built,

3. some of the skills that might help you to introduce it to a group, and reflect upon it and articulate what you're learning, and

4. some pass-on-able habits that groups who dwell in the Word have developed.

Dwelling in the Word is an intentional habit or practice. As with any habit, it takes awhile for it to become a part of your life. This pocket handbook is meant as a ready reference and a handy encouragement for you as you discover Dwelling in the Word.

Chapter 3

DWELLING IN THE WORLD

THE NEXT FEW CHAPTERS offer a view of what dwelling in the Word has meant in a variety of settings—what it looked and felt like, and what happened as a result—to a church council, to a seminary class, to an executive church body staff, and to a research, consulting, and home-team staff.

Dwelling leads to discerning mission

Congregations are blessed by God concretely, specifically. There is something about God's mission in each town that each church is called and equipped to do. Just as each Christian has a vocation, a call to participate in life as a gifted child of God, so too, each congregation has a missional vocation.

The work of leaders is figuring out what that calling is. How better to listen for it, to deliberate upon it, than by dwelling in the Word?

It is quite rare for one person to have lots of gifts—musical gifts, gifts of prayer, athletic gifts, gifts of telling the truth in love, and also gifts of hearing the God questions in others' lives. The question might be, how do you view and use the gifts you have? For each are precious.

The same might be said of a congregation.

At any one moment in time, a congregation is made up of people who together hold a particular constellation of gifts and capacities. What the congregation does well, it enjoys tremendously.

Moreover, the Spirit has a missional vocation for each of the things the congregation does well. The Spirit works to turn the gifts of the congregation outward to build community and relationship with persons who do not yet—but who desperately need to—know Jesus.

The action that naturally flows from Dwelling in the Word is Dwelling in the World. The community of Christ that is gathered and gifted is also the community of Christ that is sent. And, of course, there is no space for dwelling in the Word that isn't already dwelling in the World.

A crucial part of dwelling in the Word is listening to another. In the fourth step, we are asked to listen a reasonably friendly-looking stranger into free speech. This prepares us for listening actual strangers, people that we do not know in our community, into free speech, and in that listening, hearing the times and places God is up to something in our community—in the world.

We sometimes dwell in the World in an activity known as plunging, entering the neighborhood and listening deeply to persons we may already have fleeting connections with, listening their story into being, listening for ways their story is a part of God's story.

The deep listening connects us to another, helps us to form community with that person, that group. Over time, dwelling in the World makes the space and time in which we are transformed by the stranger's story and formed into a new community with them.

MEETINGS AS...

Decision Making   Discerning God's Will

A church council, a visioning team, a worship committee, an education task force in a local church can dwell in the Word, listen to one another and to the congregation and to God speaking in scripture, and try to answer the question, "What is God up to among us? What piece of God's action are we being fitted for now?"

At the same time they can dwell in the World, listening to their neighbors and other community partners to understand where God is already working there and which people God is calling them to learn from and form Christian community with right now. When they take up that work, they know they are participating in the very life of God.

Chapter 4

THE CASE OF THE CHURCH COUNCIL

Getting started

The new council president said she would serve on one condition: that the council dwell in the Word of God for the first 20 minutes of each meeting, staying in one passage all year: Luke 10:1-12, a missional story of pairs of followers being sent to people whom Jesus himself intends to visit.

The pastor did not object to this practice, nor did the council—mostly—although reaction was mixed. Some folks loved beginning a meeting this way because it focused them for the work the council was called to do. Others stiffened, and some even rolled their eyes. When would the real meeting start? One, after the second meeting that began this way, asked the president in front of the council exactly when the meetings would actually begin, since he preferred to attend for the decision-making.

The council followed the 6 steps, starting with the first: to pray and to read aloud. They did so, following this version of Luke 10:1-12:

After this the Lord appointed seventy others and sent them on ahead of him in pairs to every town and place where he himself intended to go. He said to them, "The harvest is plentiful, but the laborers are few; therefore ask the Lord of the harvest to send out laborers into his harvest. Go on your way. See, I am sending you out like lambs into the midst of wolves. Carry no purse, no bag, no sandals; and greet no one on the road. Whatever house you enter, first say, 'Peace to this house!' And if anyone is there who shares in peace your peace will rest on that person; but if not, it will return to you. Remain in the same house, eating and drinking whatever they provide, for the laborer deserves to be paid. Do not move about from house to house. Whenever you enter a town and its people welcome you, eat what is set before you; cure the sick who are there, and say to them, 'The kingdom of God has come near to you.' But whenever you enter a town and they do not welcome you, go out into its streets and say, 'Even the dust of your town that clings to our feet, we wipe off in protest against you. Yet know this: the kingdom of God has come near.' I tell you, on that day it will be more tolerable for Sodom than for that town. *(NRSV)*

The next step was to wrestle together over these questions: "What is God up to in this passage for us? Here? Now? What is God up to in our church and in our town?"

The first few times it was a little clunky. Who knew what God was up to, after all?

But the council members noticed there were a lot of things going on in the Bible story: pairs going out to places unknown, carrying nothing extra. They extended peace to the house they entered, looking for persons of peace there. They were utterly dependent on their hosts. They were eating, curing the sick, proclaiming with them. And that curse at the end? That was hard to keep hearing, let alone make sense of.

Something came up

At the second or third meeting, a pair of visitors came to the council with a request: They needed a new church home for a preschool. They were in some distress but hoping for hospitality. The council heard their story calmly and with interest, giving them safe haven to think about next steps. Then in pairs the council got to work studying the responses it could make.

Who knew what God was up to, after all?

25

A chance to reflect

The next month when the council read Luke 10, it was clear to many of them that Luke's story was true for *them*. A pair had come to *them*, extending the peace. They had returned it, and relationships were being formed as a result. A new church preschool was coming into being.

But there was more. The peace that the council had extended to the school also was extended to the neighboring congregation who had lost the school, and they returned the peace in a service of reconciliation. Some curing of the sick was happening, and many on the council recognized that they were in a story, and their story was part of God's story.

Meditating Alone

Discerning in Community

This is what comes of dwelling in the Word. Really living inside a story over time begins to shape a group's imagination.

Dwelling is living, sitting or waiting—together. It is listening, praying, and wondering about God's Word and God's mission—together. That's what makes it so powerful. A person can dwell alone, of course, meditating on the Word in a process of extended prayer. But dwelling in the Word is done in community. And this council was learning from each other how God was speaking, sending, coaxing, even puzzling each member.

Dwelling is not easy for some

Adopting this practice of dwelling may have been hard for those council members with a lot of Bible study experience. Folks who participate in Bible study are intrigued by the Word but may wait for the leader to interpret it for them, or offer several readings of a particular sentence. They may be looking for the historical references that would explain an image or a saying.

Dwelling in the Word involves very little of this information. Dwelling is less about learning information, as important as that is, and more about learning about one another and what God might be up to in the midst of us.

Dwelling is enveloping. It is being formed as a community of spiritual discernment within the Word of God.

Less About Information

More About What God Might Be
Up to in the Midst of Us

Dwelling was surely hard for those who were uncomfortable with silent reflection. The council members who raised objections early on were pretty sure that they had *not* been elected to sit in silent reflection. They were there to converse, study, make decisions, and manage the life of the church. They surely had no objections to the Word. They just didn't want to participate in dwelling in it every time.

Yet, as the council continued this practice using this text for a full year, many of them began to recognize things that were happening to the church as things that were happening in the life of God.

Chapter 5

THE CASE OF THE RELUCTANT SEMINARY CLASS

Getting started

There is a course at Luther Seminary called Reading the Audiences. It is a class in which first-year students learn to dig into their congregations—their history, practices, members, physical location, nearby neighbors—in order to discern what God is doing in that place and what missional vocation that congregation might have. Through the semester, the students are to become "detectives of divinity" in that place.

Imagine their surprise when, in the first class meeting, the first half hour is spent dwelling in the Word—in Philippians 1:27 and 2:5-11, the "Christ Hymn." The Christ Hymn is the dwelling passage for this course because the students will need to have the mind of Christ Jesus, the mind of a slave, on behalf of the congregation they are getting to know. Here is the passage:

Philippians 1:27, 2:5-11 (NRSV)
1:27 Only, live your life in a manner worthy of the gospel of Christ, so that, whether I come and see you or am absent and hear about you, I will know that you are standing firm in one spirit, striving side by side with one mind for the faith of the gospel.

2:5 Let the same mind be in you that was in Christ Jesus,
6 who, though he was in the form of God, did not regard equality with God as something to be exploited,
7 but emptied himself, taking the form of a slave,

being born in human likeness.

8 And being found in human form, he humbled himself and became obedient to the point of death— even death on a cross.

9 Therefore God also highly exalted him and gave him the name that is above every name,

10 So that at the name of Jesus every knee should bend, in heaven and on earth and under the earth,

11 and every tongue should confess that Jesus Christ is Lord, to the glory of God the Father.

On the first day, students are usually a little nervous or anxious, and this dwelling activity puzzles them. Most other classes dive into the syllabus and work; this is odd and seems time-consuming, especially when they have to meet a stranger and listen to what that stranger says, reporting back what that person has said without adding their own ideas. Of course it is a good way to introduce everyone in the class to everyone else, and it allows each person to participate with very little pressure, valuing every contribution equally. But this quietly reflective practice seems quite unconnected with the course's reputation for arduous work.

At the next class meeting, the students begin again by dwelling in the Word, the same passage. We explain that story is a narrative of the course and their work within it. They find a new partner and share, demonstrating their ability to listen and report without placing too much of their own reflection into that report, but they are puzzled by the return to the same text. Then they hear a lecture and they work in their groups, solving some already emerging difficulties in the congregational study they are beginning together.

At the third class meeting, the class again opens by dwelling in the Word, the same passage. They find another new partner and hear yet another view of the Christ Hymn, sometimes quite different, but sometimes both partners will have been struck by the same word or phrase and led into a conversation out of which each can hardly separate their insights from the other's. Some students ask aloud at this point, "Why this same

Bored by the Same Text?

passage every week? Surely the Scriptures are rich and this is a very limited way to explore them." Some are just wondering; others are irritated.

"Not this again!"

By the fourth or fifth class meeting, when each group member is stretched by the amount of work in this heavy course, when interviews in congregations are tough to schedule and a walk-through in the congregation's neighborhood didn't happen because someone's child was ill or someone's car didn't start, and frustrations are mounting, the class still opens by dwelling in the Word, the same passage.

Class members have met quite a few fellow students in the practice by now, listening them into free speech on the Christ Hymn and their imaginations having been caught in various places, not always agreeing but mostly listening pretty well. But it is clear that most of the students at this point would prefer having that half hour to meet and check signals with their group rather then spend time in the same passage yet again. They are frustrated with the professors for insisting upon the practice.

Also, by this time one or two students have stopped reporting the words of their partner and just begun saying what they themselves think. Someone may call them on this practice error, noting that, if they don't report their partner's insights, the group will be missing something. Even if the group is too timid to insist aloud at the moment on proper practice, they do note it when it occurs. Many times in students' private reflection papers later in the course, this failure of one student or another to dwell through the imagination of the other is noted as a loss, a deficiency, for the group.

Somewhere along about the 7th or 8th week in the semester, the completed congregational study is due. All of the frenzied work is complete, and the students begin scheduling a time when they can meet with a group of congregation leaders to share what they've learned and to ask some reflection questions of those leaders. This preparation is happening behind the scenes, the student groups working at interpreting what they have been learning as "detectives of divinity." They are to take their learnings and their questions to the congregational group as slaves to the congregation, slaves who, by their work, free the congregation members to see their church in a new way, see their church as newcomers see it, see potential missional vocations and what God might be up to in the congregation and in the community outside its walls.

The Case of the Reluctant Seminary Class

First Week — Surprised

Second Week — Puzzled

Third Week — Irritated

A Few Weeks Later — Open & Curious

Still, at the start of each class meeting, the class opens by dwelling in the Word, the same passage. And it is at this point (for one or two students it happens a week or so earlier) that several students will dwell, remain silent, open, in extended prayer, and then share with the class the word at which they were "caught" by the Spirit. In fact, their tone has changed. They are surprised but delighted that this one story is still "catching" them, and in unexpected ways. They cannot believe it has so much to say, especially given that the passage is not strange to them; they had already heard it many times even before that first class period. But it is only now that they begin to be curious about where and how it is striking others in the class. They hear familiar patterns and new ones, too. They see the various theological lines of their class-mates working, working, working through the story of Jesus' slavehood to human beings. They grapple with the baggage that the word *slave* brings with it, they know one another well enough to argue a little about that, and the 30-minute practice sometimes swells to 40 or 50 minutes.

Taking the practice to others

Finally it is time for each student group to make a formal presentation and conversation with the members of the church they have been learning about. Many of those groups begin that meeting by dwelling in the Word, the same passage. And they are sometimes confronted by church members cutting them off, saying, "We came for a presentation. What is this Bible study?"

The students are surprised, but they behave as slave to their congregation's members, delivering to them what they learned in the project and inviting the church members to interact, provide more knowledge, fill in blanks, and even respond to theological reflection questions about what God may be up to in their church and neighborhood. Some of the church members never understand the students' purpose in dwelling in the Word (not the same as Bible study), but others see the connection.

At last, the students present to the class about their meeting with the congregation and what they learned. They also write a reflection paper about the process, and sometimes Dwelling in the Word figures in these pieces of their work, especially if they've tried to do it with the church leaders and either succeeded or failed.

A chance to reflect

Students also write a final paper on missional leadership and what God is up to. And in at least 70% of the papers, Dwelling in the Word is mentioned as a rich and simple practice that students have learned bears fruit for them in their group work and in their personal lives. They mention their original reluctance to stay in the same story, until the story takes them over and becomes their story and they become part of Christ's story.

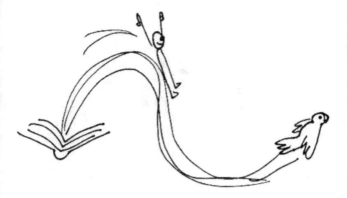

Becoming Part of Christ's Story

In the end, they don't believe this would have happened if the class had hopped around into various passages. And they can see how it draws all people in to participate without placing much of a burden on them, no matter their native language or level of education, for one reflection may have as much insight as another. Just as in the Christ hymn, Christ opens up the community of God to all people, so they open up the community of believers to all people through this hospitable and welcoming practice. They live the Christ Hymn by dwelling in it.

Chapter 6

THE CASE OF THE EXECUTIVE CHURCH BODY STAFF

Getting started

"You know, we really appreciate the chance to begin these retreats in the Word of God. There is so much of the Word of God. Really a lot of it. Sixty-six books of it."

"Yes, it is deep and rich with so many stories. Parables, even."

"So aren't we limiting ourselves by staying in Luke 10:1-12 for each of our retreats? Limiting what we can learn from the Word?"

These comments came from three members of a large judicatory staff near the start of their second staff covenanting retreat. At the first retreat a month earlier, they had been polite and gone along with the practice. When they realized that at the second retreat they would dwell in the same passage, they were a little irritated, perhaps even bored, with Luke 10.

Understandable. Staying in the Luke 10:1-12 passage for three retreats during a staff covenanting process seemed quite limiting, especially given the extensive work they were doing between retreats. After all, staff covenanting takes several months, involves self-discovery, team discovery and a lot of homework. And they do all of this with only Luke 10:1-12 as their companion.

And so, there were suggestions. Perhaps there could be a different text for each of the retreats. Or maybe each person could choose a different verse upon which to base their own work.

Freeing others into free speech

Of course some members of this particular staff saw the value of the exercise in deep listening, of dwelling with a partner.

Without this partner exercise at the first retreat, executive staff members and maybe one or two others would have been the only ones to speak, to volunteer any comments on the passage—at least, they were the only ones to speak up during any other of that retreat's conversations.

But the dwelling exercise helps change that. It puts individuals in pairs with someone they aren't usually paired with. It has each person getting to know another's thoughts and reactions. It has each person trying on another person's understanding of or questions about the scripture. It has each person repeating to the whole group what their partner has said.

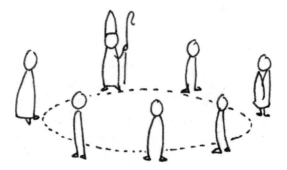

Circle of Conversation and Perspective

In terms of group dynamics or psychology, one could call this pairing "perspective taking," since each person must report the perspective of the other. In asymmetrical relationships, such as a bishop with a maintenance manager, the power of learning from another can be very great, even unexpectedly great. The maintenance manager may simply expect to learn from an executive leader's reaction to Luke 10:1-12, and speak the bishop's words to the group the way a person repeats an answer in a class taught by a professor. But when an executive leader takes the maintenance manager's words and reports them to the group, having heard something new and profound in the story, a power shift occurs in the dynamic; we see power, servanthood, even slavehood for the sake of hearing the other clearly.

But something else happened as these staff members listened one another into free speech as the group dwelled in the Word. On this executive church body staff, some members were very new, while others had been in the system for decades. When we took up Luke 10:1-12, one of the newer persons would note the missional aspect of the journey Jesus was sending the pairs to make, as well as the style of the instructions for that journey:

> "What a lot of specific instructions! Jesus was very specific about what he wanted them to do and say, wasn't he!"

> "Wow! They were embarking on this trip with someone else and they had almost *no* clues about

what to do or say and took nothing with them. I can't imagine doing that!"

Then long-time system members responded to such comments, noting how nice it would have been to have had such instructions when assuming *their* offices some years back. Quietly the long-timers took note of which newcomers valued specific instructions and which desired more open-ended ones, learning much about one another in the act of taking up the Word.

Where Metaphors and Images Dance

But why should we remain in the same house?

But back to the objections to the practice of remaining in just one passage. Surely all of scripture has much, much, much to offer, and staying in Luke 10 does limit a staff to one set of images and information. Yes. It limits the information. It gives a certain set of boundaries. It creates a set of walls and windows. It makes a space within which several metaphors and images dance.

It confines, it forms in a certain way, the information for a group of people, and through that confinement, formation, and focus, they begin to see everything differently, by the power of the Holy Spirit as it opens the imaginations of everyone in that metaphoric place. By the time a group has "remained in the same house," as Luke 10:5 instructs, several times, these metaphors and images, just a few of them, begin to dance with the thoughts and reflections of the staff participants.

That is the remarkable thing. Dwelling in the Word is not about getting information from the Word, information to be used or applied to our job authorizations or work planning. A staff dwells in the Word in order to create a space for the Spirit to teach us, to help us teach one another, to form Christian community and base it in the Word. In fact, it gives them the time and space as they work together to call for the Gospel in their midst.

Not at first, but often by the second day of that retreat, someone, not usually one of the positional leaders like a moderator, bishop, or executive, but rather one of the support persons such as the website designer or the communication assistant, will surprise the group by drawing them all back to the Word. Here's how it happened on this staff.

Staff members were working through the staff covenanting 3-column list: descriptions of what each person (1) feels *responsible* to do in any given week, (2) feels *authorized* to do (given the actual time, money, and access to get done), and (3) *wants someday to be authorized* to do. The person who coordinated this particular church body's print news, website, and materials for assemblies was comparing his *responsible* column and his *authorized* column.

He said, "Well, these ten things are my responsibilities from my job description, but I also feel authorized to do these ten things, as if I had been given instructions and sent out to get them done—kind of like in Luke 10. I even have a partner—like being sent in a pair!—to get numbers 6 to 8 done."

"Yes! *Pairs* are in Luke 10, too!" said the treasurer.

"Yes, and that makes me wonder," said the executive, "how many times we actually do work in pairs without really acknowledging it."

And so on.

While remaining in one passage does limit information and the number of stories or characters to learn from, the images and metaphors that *are* present in that one passage begin to seep into people's thinking and reflection and begin to show the staff members how even their most ordinary work may be grounded in scripture, may be seen as a mission in the same way the "70 others" had a mission. Staying in Luke 10 creates conditions that encourage a missional imagination. And that, we believe, is a work of the Spirit, revealing how people are acting within the life of God.

Recall the series of objections to remaining in Luke 10? These objections always arise at the second retreat, when it becomes clear that the consultants are going to stay there and not move. You will have noticed that it always happens in class, too, about the third or fourth week, and that it always happens in council or session or committee meetings, too. As soon as people see that it's not a perfunctory devotional activity or Bible study done for application to life, dwelling starts to feel like a habit, and many people are disinterested in having (and sometimes downright opposed to having) this habit.

Of course it is a habit. When you have to sit still and listen to the same Word, and hear it through the imagination of another, reporting back what the other

46

thinks and not what you think, it may also seem like a lot of bother. It may even seem dangerous. And it is. And how it transforms.

On the third retreat, this church body staff arrived and settled in for the opening Dwelling in the Word. Someone volunteered to read, they observed some silence, and then they found a partner, although many had partnered with one another before by this time in the cycle. There was an energy, almost a pressing forward, an eagerness to hear what everyone was about to say *this time*. And oddly, while the one person reported the words of the partner, people looked at not just the reporter but the partner as well, as if they were hearing them both speak at the same time. Partners checked with one another to see whether they'd reported faithfully, the conversation got lively, and it was nearly impossible to move to the next item of work on the retreat schedule.

The staff members seemed taken up into the passage—they were hearing it and understanding much more, and it was speaking to parts of their lives no one could have anticipated in the first or second retreats. Not only that, the staff seemed much less asymmetrical when dwelling than they did any other time. After all, no matter who you are, when you are Dwelling in the Word in this way, you are at the service of the other you are hearing.

On pausing to be taken up into the life of God

Life on a church body staff has real pressure. People have demanding schedules, and they provide types of support to congregations that they never dreamed of when they began doing the work. They share the joys and woes of one another's lives, they are often subject to very dirty politics, they live in glass houses, and they need to trust one another and trust the One who has called them into such work on behalf of others.

Dwelling in the Word helps a church body staff see that the power of the Holy Spirit is as real and as close as their practice of Dwelling in the Word together. It shows them that God's Word, although containing 66 books of wisdom, is not there just to give them information. It is alive, and it witnesses to the power of the Triune God every time they make room in their lives for it to do so.

The Spirit calls them together, presents the passage, one which they have learned well enough to recite from memory, and then surprises them with God's own power and images and their own recollections of what they've heard and seen in the past week, making it new, alive: the *viva vox*. The Spirit creates with them Christian community, a body where trust lives and where loving and serving the other is the way to live. How they dwell together in the Word determines how they *dwell together*.

Chapter 7

THE CASE OF
THE RESEARCH, CONSULTING,
AND HOME-TEAM STAFF

Getting started

The staff at Church Innovations Institute has ebbed and flowed during our 25 years. We have had several different people serve as executive director, office manager, and operations manager, and many different research associates and consultants. But since 1997—for more than 15 years—we have had only one dwelling text: Luke 10: 1-12.

This text is the passage associated in the Episcopal Church USA with David Oakerhater, an early Episcopal Native American evangelist and missionary.

Your authors were attending a retreat weekend with some leaders from the Minnesota Council on Indian Work of the Episcopal Diocese of Minnesota, exactly on David Oakerhater's Day 1997 to plan some work on resources for lay catechists. Every morning we read the passage, we heard it at lunch and at other times of the day, and we closed the evening with it. It shaped the flow of our planning and began to shape our imaginations.

At the close of the weekend, those Native American Episcopal leaders said to us, "This should be your dwelling story at Church Innovations. You are always sending out or being sent; you are on God's mission." So we took the passage and the habit back to our staff. At every staff meeting, we read the passage. We read it in multiple translations of the Bible. We had different people read aloud each week. We allowed silence to unfold. We began sharing with one another (as strangers) where our imaginations got caught.

After some time, we stopped pairing and reporting our stranger's words, since after a few weeks we already had paired with everyone else there, our early staff being only 4-6 persons and our discussions being fairly lively anyway. Whenever we had a group of visitors or new consultants or students present, we added the pairing dimension of the exercise back in.

After a year or so, several of us who do consulting work on the road had introduced the practice in other places, and when the passage was read the following week at the home-team staff meeting, we often reported on the unusual new interpretations and experiences that had happened the previous week on the road. Sometimes we heard tales of a conflicted and anxious staff who had found new insight during a dwelling session. Sometimes we heard about an entire church assembly of 800 persons dwelling together around tables of 10, and how the dwelling took people out of a fighting posture and into a listening one.

But why keep this up for years?

Some of our own staff found dwelling to be a waste of time. To be sure, they valued the importance of the Word of God and the place of the scriptures in our mutual work, but we had so little face-to-face time with one another that they wondered whether dwelling was a waste of those valuable moments. When at first they sensed the high commitment of most of the group to the work, they simply remained silent, hoping others would take the hint and do the same, not speaking and so not prolonging the discussion any more than necessary.

As time progressed, they began to present such

powerful negative body language in their silence that one staff member described it feeling as though someone had turned down the thermostat 40 degrees. Indeed, the combination of silence and body language created tremendous discomfort for several staff members. Only after direct confrontation were we able to surface these staff persons' sense of our wasting time. This proved a most helpful and challenging conversation about the habit of Dwelling in the Word and about our ways of working with one another.

About the same time, part of our home-team staff decided we had probably been too long in Luke 10:1-12. We hadn't made sense out of the harsh ending but we were not likely to come to any agreement about it, we had shared many of the same images multiple times, and they felt perhaps we should move along to a different text.

The new text was chosen, and we moved. For some, this move was a good thing, at least for the first week or two. For others, it felt like being uprooted and placed in a strange apartment. We tried the new text for a month, but most of the group began referencing Luke 10, even while reading from the new text. We were longing for home. So those who had suggested the change graciously agreed to move back to Luke 10. We have never left it again.

This chapter is a description of some of the things we have learned in the process of dwelling in this Word, things that have profoundly shaped who we are at Church Innovations.

Luke 10: 1-12
[1] After this the Lord appointed seventy others and sent them on ahead of him in pairs to every town and place where he himself intended to go.

In Pairs

At some point we noticed that the Lord sent people out in pairs.

We also noticed, after months and months of reporting our work to one another, that we did better when *we* went out in pairs. We were more responsive to the people who had invited us, we were sharper, and we learned more when we were in a pair than when we were alone. It even worked when one of us went alone and then paired up with a person on the staff or in the church body or congregation that had invited us. Maybe we had always known that two heads are better than one, but one week during dwelling someone on the staff said, "Well, of course you did good work last week in that meeting. There were two of you. Even the Lord sends people out in pairs!"

"Well, of course," you might respond, "of course that's true." But until that moment we had not thought of pairing as a way to do better the work God had already given us to do. Now it has become part of our vision of our work.

> [2] He said to them, "The harvest is plentiful, but the laborers are few; therefore ask the Lord of the harvest to send out laborers into his harvest.

Some of our staff come from farming families. This image of the Lord of the harvest has always been a very powerful image for them. To see the Lord of the harvest, standing at the edge of his harvest field, noting how few the laborers are, had the power to make us very sad. And then one day someone said, "But look! It's our job to pray to that same Lord of the harvest for laborers. Let's do that!"

Ask the Lord

And we began to pray for laborers. Sometimes it was for a laborer to join our own staff in a particular capacity. Sometimes it was for laborers in the Church at large. And sometimes it was for a very specific laborer for one of the groups we were consulting with.

We do not know how many times this has happened, but we can remember a dozen times that, much later on, after hiring a new staff person or hearing of someone joining a project or staff we had been consulting with, someone said, "Hmm. That must be what happens when we pray to the Lord of the harvest." We don't even realize the effect at the moment, but the Lord sends the laborers as we pray for them.

> [3] Go on your way. See, I am sending you out like lambs into the midst of wolves.

From time to time, the Church Innovations staff has felt, like most people, like lambs in the midst of wolves.

As individuals, we have run into our share of hostile people, people who look like the enemy, people who take *us* to be the enemy, people who are ready to eat and who see us as tasty morsels to put away.

Like Lambs into the Midst of Wolves

Recently during dwelling at our home-team staff meeting, one of our members brought back from the road a beautiful new image: the wolves are ravenous, all right, but they are hungry for something they have never experienced—the full love of God in Christ Jesus. And Jesus the Lamb, in us, is what they seek. They do not seek so much to devour us as to gain Jesus.

What a difference it makes to a researcher, to a consultant, to the staff of an organization that partners with church bodies through change and conflict, to think of ourselves as bringing Christ as a Lamb to those who are hungry and cannot be satisfied with anything else.

> [4] Carry no purse, no bag, no sandals; and greet no one on the road.

Of course we have some fun with this verse on the road when we are having trouble dealing with luggage. But the notion of going just as we are—to be completely dependent on our host's hospitality, to come mostly to listen and learn, then eat and cure—is very hard to do at first, especially when we are consultants hired with the expectation that we will come bearing solutions to their every problem. Early on, even we believed we had to come up with all the solutions.

And then this passage opened our eyes. The Holy Spirit had given every town and place where Jesus intends to go all the resources it needs. We bring only ourselves to that place and spend our time there accepting the gifts of the host. In focusing only on the host and not on what we bring, we prepare for the work ahead of us.

> [5] Whatever house you enter, first say, 'Peace to this house!' [6] And if anyone is there who shares in peace your peace will rest on that person; but if not, it will return to you.

Over the years we have spent a lot of time wondering what it looks like to extend the peace and see it rest on someone. And, in turn, eventually most of us have seen it happen and told stories of actually knowing where it rested. We were able to depend on that peace and that person when the work got difficult. We also see ourselves as the hosts in the story, offering hospitality. Of course we have wondered then how many times someone has actually extended the peace to *us* and did not see it rest upon someone on our staff. Then what? At least the guest does not go away empty-handed, since our Lord promises that the peace will return to them. But whichever way we see ourselves in the story, this verse gives us pause.

> ⁷ Remain in the same house, eating and drinking whatever they provide, for the laborer deserves to be paid. Do not move about from house to house.

We have had an ambivalent relationship with this verse. It tells us to eat, for the laborer deserves to be paid, and we love that because we work hard for those who invite us to be partners with them.

Eat and Drink Whatever They Provide

But it also tells us to remain in the same house and not move about, even though we are always seeking (and the Lord is always delivering) new relationships. We have come to believe that some verses, like this one, keep us always trying to discern the Spirit's calling for us. Our best work has often been the long-term walk with a church body through change and trial. Perhaps this verse tells us to be in the relationship for the long haul and not simply for convenience's sake.

> [8] Whenever you enter a town and its people welcome you, eat what is set before you; [9] cure the sick who are there, and say to them, 'The kingdom of God has come near to you.'

Once again, eating! Eating is seldom a problem for our research and consulting staff. Of course, we have been invited to many places where the food is unlike anything we've ever had before. Sometimes the food or the language or the customs or the culture is so different as to be very uncomfortable—painful, even.

Yet if we do not sit with our hosts, eat with them, *be* with them, how can we know them? How can we walk with them through the challenges they face? Whether this is the curing of the sick, we are not sure. But we are not reluctant to mention that God's kingdom has come near to our hosts, that God has a preferred and promised future for them, and that the Holy Spirit has given all the necessary clues to discern it. God's kingdom is indeed near.

> [10] But whenever you enter a town and they do not welcome you, go out into its streets and say, [11] 'Even the dust of your town that clings to our feet, we wipe off in protest against you. Yet know this: the kingdom of God has come near.' [12] I tell you, on that day it will be more tolerable for Sodom than for that town. *(NRSV)*

Now, of course for many mainline Christians, this ending can be troubling. We have gone over it and over it. We have wondered at the harshness of it. We have become frightened at the power of the sent ones to curse a whole town if they are not welcomed properly. We have noted that the proclamation is the same whether they are welcomed or not, but even that wisdom does not lighten very much the heaviness of the ending.

We are not alone in that wondering. More than once we have brought Luke 10:1-12 to a large event, given it to someone to reproduce for projection, and begun to lead Dwelling in the Word only to discover that they have stopped the passage early at verse 11 or even at verse 9, leaving off the ending. When asked about this editing later, the person will always say, "Oh, that taste is just too sour," or "Oh, we don't want to go *there*, do we?" or "Please. Not every line of Scripture is important."

But somehow, all 12 verses have been teaching us for these many years. Even the last three verses. They give urgency to our task. They tell us not to linger if we're not welcome. They tell us that we won't succeed at everything and that we must move on. They even tell us that the curse, if it's the only thing some people in that town or place hear, may be the very way that the Spirit will get those people's attention. And so we wrestle on.

On our home-team staff, our research consortium, our consultants group, and our Board, we have Roman Catholics, Lutherans, Presbyterians, United Methodists, Covenanters, Baptists, Mennonites, Episcopalians and Anglicans, Uniting Reformed, Dutch Reformed,

Reformed Church of America, Evangelicals, several other denominations, and fellowships of congregations as well as independent churches. We also have hybrids of these and one or two persons who would never identify with any of these.

And yet, all participate in Dwelling in the Word. The habit of dwelling creates for us a story in which we are all speaking the same language, in which each of us plays a part, sometimes a different part every time we read it together. It shapes us, placing us into God's story. In this habit, we experience our work together as one way we dwell in the life of God.

Chapter 8

LEADING, KILLING, AND BEING LIBERATED

HOW DOES ONE LEAP from stories of groups who dwelt in the Word to killing and being liberated? It seems like quite a stretch. But there's a reason to take a moment to think about death and freedom here.

Your two authors have probably led Dwelling in the Word in more places and times with more people and in more diversity of cultures than almost anyone we know, making more mistakes than anyone we know! More interestingly, we have watched more people lead Dwelling in the Word than anyone else has. We hope to share in this chapter a few lessons about leading Dwelling in the Word. We will also have to describe the ways of leading that kill the process and the ways of leading that often lead to being liberated by the Spirit.

Leading

You never know who is going to be a leader in Dwelling in the Word. This early discovery remains one of the most important. In most local churches, people place leadership regarding the scriptures either into the hands of professional ministers or of a select few local leaders who are accustomed to speaking in front of others or who have certain expertise or education. But the way that dwelling in the Word works makes it possible for persons who are not usually thought of as leaders to lead in dwelling.

A Risk

Picture a group of working class women chosen to deliver a major research report that they had helped to build to their church council and staff. They were quite uncomfortable at the thought of presenting before an essentially male leadership group. However, they had been practicing dwelling in the Word within their own group during their work of doing interviews and creating this report. So they began their presentation by dwelling in the Word.

This beginning created a new set of power relationships and dynamics. Those who normally controlled the conversation (the council members) were freed to explore God's Word for themselves and for their local church without having to also lead or control the conversation. The group of women who led the dwelling in the Word felt no need or pressure for the group to come to answers, but rather were delighted at the chance to free the council to explore God's Word.

Two wonderful things happened as a result: First, the women experienced the power of being servants to the more traditional leadership as an important energy for leading, and second, the council discovered a whole new leadership base and resource right under their noses.

One might take from this story a false impression that the secret to dwelling in the Word is to have no leadership at all; that is, to abdicate the place of leadership in order to create the space and time for the conversation and to simply guide it. Quite often stories like this one get romanticized into the rather silly claim that anyone can lead because effective leadership is simply letting go. That claim undermines the extraordinary leadership capacity of these ordinary women.

Quite to the contrary, these women had well-developed capacities to be servants who free others to dwell in the Word. They had been practicing the components of those capacities for months. Many of them had honed several of those capacities in lives of service to others. They came with many of those components well in place from lives that had allowed them very few leader roles. And the occasion of leading dwelling in the Word with the church council freed them to exercise these capacities in a place and time in which they previously would never have been invited to lead. They had learned from hard experience and deliberate practice what it took to lead in this setting.

Leadership Regarding the Scripture

One of the most important insights they had was learning to trust the Holy Spirit. They came with the attitude and belief that wherever two or more are gathered in Jesus' name, Jesus' promise of the Spirit of the Risen and ascended Lord, the Holy Spirit, will be true. They came with the minimum knowledge base about how to read a text out loud and invite people to dwell in it. They came with useful skills that they had been practicing for months as they had completed interviews in their congregation. They were prepared to pass those habits on to the group of traditional church leaders. Their work was not the abdication of leadership; it *was* leadership within the Spirit and promises of the Triune God.

Killing

Christian innovation is a process of failure growing out of a Christian imagination and wisdom towards a shared positive outcome. Some experiences of dwelling in the Word can illustrate very painfully this hard process of failure.

Taking Notes

Picture a room quieted after hearing the Word read aloud. Then silence, right? No, not silence. Hear it? Clickety clickety click. It was the sound of a laptop keyboard, the result of the Stated Clerk's taking of notes continuously during a time of dwelling in the Word at a big presbytery meeting. The Stated Clerk's separation from the process, keeping distance from the dwelling, indeed the clerk's polished refusal to participate in the dwelling, was only the first indicator of a set of practices in this group that made dwelling almost impossible.

The second indicator of failure was that members of the presbytery were unwilling to seek out a reasonably friendly-looking stranger and move over to listen. With the announcement that "everybody knows one another here," everyone in the various factions of the presbytery stayed seated where they were and refused to move.

The third indicator of failure was the first person's report back to the large group after working with her "reasonably friendly-looking stranger." Her report was all about what she thought; it simply stated her own reading of the text, not her friendly-looking stranger's. In fact, during their time of listening one another into free speech, they had succeeded mostly in questioning the value of anything that the Apostle Paul might say to us from Philippians because of his sexism and racism.

Everyone after that first person followed suit, not reporting what they had heard but piling onto the initial suspicions of Paul. The Philippians text had not been arbitrarily brought to the presbytery that night out of the blue, either; no, the Philippians text had been chosen *by the presbytery* as the key text for their visioning and planning process, their purpose for meeting. Well, the dwelling went downhill from there. The anxiety in the group went up. The visioning and planning process never recovered. We fired ourselves. We had extended the peace and we were not welcome.

Of course the role of the Stated Clerk is to take very good notes on every topic under discussion and order those notes for the presbytery for future reference. Effective leaders of dwelling might well have underlined to the group the importance of *everyone's* fully participating in the dwelling, of not taking notes but letting the talking and listening flow. Effective leaders also might well have intervened when people claimed they already knew one another and didn't need to move and seek out someone new. Effective leaders surely should have intervened when it was clear that the first report back was not a report of listening to another but of someone's own opinions. If the leaders of dwelling had made any of those interventions, they might have prevented the total failure of the dwelling. Of course, the power structures of the presbytery were being threatened severely by the dwelling in the Word process. By calling attention to what was not happening, leaders might also have only precipitated a much too early confrontation on the structural dysfunctions. Still, true servants of dwelling in the

Word must risk such confrontation. Leadership comes with *real* risk.

One of the simplest lessons here is how the practices of leadership in the church in its most modern forms actually are threatened by dwelling in the Word. This failure to dwell well was not an accident but rather a whole series of failures arising from deeply-held rules for the use of scripture by leaders in the church. For example, these good and faithful people held the *modern* belief in using distance in order to stay objective; that explained the Stated Clerk's continuous clicking. He understood that his role was to remain outside, objective, in order to effectively balance the different power interests in the presbytery and provide clear records of what happened. Needless to say, dwelling in the Word suggests a different understanding of power and its exercise, even though the Stated Clerk's place in other parts of the meeting might well return to recording and ordering information for the good of the group.

Another simple lesson from this example is the role of critical suspicions. In Dwelling in the Word, leaders deliberately use the *postmodern* invitation to begin with an interpretive stance of *good will*, an invitation for participants to open themselves hospitably to whatever they hear in the Word and from one another. In this practice everyone enters a space and time of seeking to hear God's Word through listening one another into free speech, listening to everyone, including both the persons in the room and the author of the text. As time goes on in the habit of dwelling, there is plenty of space to bring forward important and even critical suspicions. But if we *start* from an interpretive stance of *suspicion*, that classical modern way of hearing kills our dwelling together. "The letter kills; the Spirit gives life."

Actually, the ways of killing dwelling in the Word are myriad. On one occasion when leading a dwelling in the Word, a man with a degree in systematic theology and hermeneutics very early on in the dwelling started to show off his in-depth knowledge of a critical reading of the text. A number of other well-read persons in the room took the cue and began to do the same. Needless to say, the dwelling in the Word did not lead to a floated conversation based on deep listening to the stranger's view. It didn't take long for it to sink into an "I know more than you know" dark hole.

One of the points of this tale is *not* to completely avoid critical tools and knowledge in dwelling. On the contrary, it is a question of timing. Allowing the conversation to float within a healthy spirit of good will actually creates the space and time for a more critical analysis of our understanding of scripture. Without good will, the willingness to acknowledge and assent to others' interpretations, we will have no community in which to critically assess those readings.

Also, we must underline that this tale is *not* meant to reject the modern Bible study. Bible study in its many forms should be supported. However, this tale does illustrate that dwelling is a very special framing of Bible study within an interpretive and communal good will.

Part of the genuine challenge in a diverse culture—where we cannot depend on always having a shared set of values and meanings—is that, if we begin with suspicion, we will almost certainly kill conversation. However, if we begin with assent and good will, we likely create a conversation that gives life, energy, and multiple ways to look at tough critical questions.

Good Bible study must have the critical distance to support such critical questions, but without the framework, the setting, the environment of a community working from assent and good will, there's no one who will speak up. Or if someone does, he or she may do so to provide "the one right answer" and squelch conversation in the Spirit, even unintentionally. In effect, too much of modern Bible study creates smaller and smaller niches of folks who agree with one another, small groups of people who confirm their own prejudices, and hide that action under the mask of the good and important work of being critically suspicious.

Smaller and Smaller Niches

Leadership that gives life to Christian community invites people to good will and assent borne by trusting the Holy Spirit. This is leadership with real risk that leads to innovation.

Of course actions that can kill true dwelling in the Word are not always purely related to modern attitudes and academic learning. You already know that there are some very old power moves that are almost impossible to criticize (or recover from) in the church.

Our favorite example of such an action is "The Pious Power Move." You may have seen this one. For example, when a tough conversation is underway and several people have offered differing and sometimes conflicting interpretations, people's anxiety rises. It is very tempting for an anxious person to use a pious power move like this one: "What's really important is that God is love, and so we shouldn't dwell on these differences. Let's just love one another." Where does that leave the persons who were putting their minds and hearts into true listening and reporting back various interpretations?

Or, worse, as the anxiety rises, some people are very tempted to say, "Wait! Let's pray. Right now." Of course, prayer is very much related to dwelling in the Word. In fact, as the habit of dwelling develops, it often becomes extended prayer, especially if longer and longer silence is allowed to unfold before people move to listening to a stranger. But when someone jumps into a developing conversation filled with differences and requests prayer out of anxiety, that move actually demeans the differences between good people and breaks things up just as important understandings are almost in hand.

Being liberated

When all is said, done, reflected on, and articulated, most of the time in dwelling in the Word we have experienced groups and individuals being liberated.

One Presbyterian student who was quite pious in

very appropriate ways, wondered aloud in class about whether there was any place for critical studies and suspicions in the habit of Dwelling in the Word. She had found the process to that point quite liberating and energizing, in contrast to many negative conversations in her adult life that had started with critical suspicions. However, as the weeks of class went by and in our weekly dwelling many students brought forward historical and critical studies and suspicions, she began to see how liberating the practice was for hearing God's Word in, with, and under the ugly facts of racism, classism, sexism, and the many other ways sin has deformed the church's reading of scripture.

Another Presbyterian student of African-American descent, who had worked in human services for the state for more than a decade, was stunned in the early stages of the Dwelling in the Word. She put it quite succinctly, "I have never been in a group of people who honored an ancient text so much!" She was *not* making a compliment. As the weeks passed, she saw how a community was being formed in the dwelling process that allowed her and others to speak honestly about some of the perverse ways the church has read and interpreted scripture. Her voice and life experience enjoyed a freer space and time than she had been used to in any diverse setting outside a group that already agreed with her. In the end she said, "I have experienced a freedom here, dwelling in this ancient text, that I have never experienced before."

One of the pitfalls of having very delightful experiences of dwelling in the Word is that you don't always get them. We become spoiled from the good ones, and then we have one that feels very flat. When this happens, we have been very tempted to retell the stories of the delightful experiences of other groups as a way of rescuing a failure.

Let Loose

We have learned the hard way that such sharing of previous "successes" seldom can turn around a bad or even just flat experience of dwelling, for a number of reasons. Instead, we have learned to feel free to trust the Holy Spirit and allow even the bad and the flat conversations their place in forming Christian conversation. Here the liberation goes two ways, as it often does. The leader lets go and feels free to allow failure as a part of innovation, and the gathered group lets go to see where they will be led. Over time these experiences actually prove powerful, both in forming community and in innovating missional church.

Over the years we have worked with many extremely gifted consultants and facilitators. Many of these have not taken to dwelling in the Word easily. Most have learned their consulting and facilitating skills in the school of modern control. That is, they have developed well-honed practices for always staying in control of a group and a conversation. When we ask them to begin each meeting of a group by dwelling in the Word, the consultant or facilitator who usually uses modern control leadership is put at uncomfortably high risk. As a result, when we invite them to lead dwelling in the Word, they almost always add other techniques and practices that they presume add value, value worthy of their expertise and cost. But in the end these added facilitation techniques also add control measures that prevent the freedom of dwelling in the Word.

We remember in particular two world-class consultants who began this way, adding techniques and instructions and frameworks to dwelling. One of them eventually took the risk of moving beyond the modern wisdom of adding high-control techniques and practices. His colleague, an equally extraordinarily gifted consultant, simply could not trust the process of dwelling and was constantly at odds with all of our consulting methods, since they all grow out of dwelling in the Word. No doubt he adds real value to the local churches and organizations with whom he consults. Equally without much doubt, the man who was able to let go of the high-control techniques and practices, especially around the scriptures, has enjoyed a kind of liberation he never expected.

We could go on with stories of leadership, killing, and being liberated; no doubt you could add many stories of your own. We share our stories both as lessons for the wise and as signs of hope for those who are seeking such dwelling in the Word. All of them serve to underline the real risk and even more amazing results when we trust the Holy Spirit in our reading of scripture.

In the beginning, middle, and end of leadership is the spiritual discipline of having the same mind that was in Christ. This is leadership that involves self-doubt. This self-doubt goes beyond a false humility. It goes to genuine recognition of the profound complexity of each of us and the perverse dangers in leadership of any kind, even leadership from below, leadership that takes the servant role. Only Jesus could have truly and fully emptied himself to the form of a slave, to obedience unto death for the other, and he did so in the power of the Holy Spirit and the will of the Father. We depend only feebly, incompletely, in this emptying. Of course, like Jesus, depending upon the same Triune God. For us the journey involves such deathly risk, too: risk in the Spirit of the living, liberating God.

Chapter 9

HOW WILL YOUR GROUP DWELL IN THE WORD?

WHAT WILL DWELLING IN THE WORD be like for your group?

Imagine how you will introduce it. What will you say? What "props" might you use? What will you have available in the room to make it easier to try?

How will you invite everyone to try it? What do you expect people's reaction will be? How long will you propose to try it out with this first group?

What passage will you use? Do you already have a text that your group identifies with? Or will you use Luke 10:1-12? Or perhaps Philippians 1:27, 2:5-11?

The Luke passage is absolutely delightful in its introduction to being missional. It is a story of 35 pairs of good people, without any training, launched out to extend the peace to people they haven't met but whom the Lord also intends to visit. It captures and eventually shapes the imagination of people who may want to look beyond their own circles into the world that God loves and to persons God wants to embrace. It provides words and images for people who want to discover how God might be calling and sending *them* to serve others.

The Philippians passage is also a story. It is Jesus' story as the first century church must have recited it week after week and month after month. It is the good news, the Gospel, for sure. But it is also very good Law. It encourages believers to be slaves to another person in order to free that other person into relationship with God through Christ Jesus by the power of the Holy Spirit. It urges the posture of slavehood or servanthood in order to free someone else. That is mission, too! And it helps, by the Holy Spirit's power, to create the community needed to tackle a tough issue without killing one another.

Once the habit settles in with most of the group, how will you introduce it to newcomers? How will you decide what value it brings to you, in order to say what value it might bring to other groups in your congregation? Remember, as in all things, people do not learn from experience. People learn from reflecting upon their experience, and articulating what they learn. They do this best together, in the group that has practiced dwelling in the Word together.

This taking time for reflection is very, very important. How will you lead by giving people a chance to reflect on what the Spirit is doing with you in dwelling in the Word? Real leadership is often about framing things, about creating time and space for people to reflect on little parts of the big picture in order to name and claim what they already know and to identify what has to be learned before a decision can be reached. Reflection allows a group to harvest what God has already given them. Your group no doubt has the capacities to dwell in the Word. Once they've done it for a time, lead them in reflecting on its value.

How will you build curiosity into the group so that members begin looking for places the Spirit is speaking to the group? How will you make it safer for people to begin speaking with one another about God's presence and activity in your midst? In our work with hundreds of congregations, no matter the denomination or continent, we have been amazed at the absence of "God talk" in one-on-one interviews, comparatively safe encounters, even when an interview question asks where God is present in congregational life. In one large set of interviews in which over 35,000 words were recorded, fewer than 90 were the words *God, Jesus* or *Christ,* or *the Holy*

Spirit. While that figure might amaze you, it didn't shock us. "God talk" in modern culture is extremely private. Many fear exposure and shame. Many rightly have critical suspicions of doing harm. Many rightly fear spiritual abuse, having experienced it. For good and bad reasons, people have just not been given permission, habits, or safe enough space to talk about what God is up to in their lives and in their shared life as congregations. Dwelling in the Word is one way to give that permission, habit, and safer space for God talk. Dwelling creates the kind of community where such talk can be accepted with good will and even tested critically. Indeed, people are apt to "speak the truth in love" only where such community has been formed by the Spirit.

We know, because people have told us many times, that the habit of Dwelling in the Word can profoundly change the shape of committee meetings, staff meetings, council, session or vestry meetings. And exactly because it changes things and allows the Spirit some elbow room, it will make people uncomfortable. That's understandable. And the people who are made uncomfortable are not bad people. They're just not used to doing this sort of spiritual discernment. Leading a group into this habit may get difficult. But take the step anyway. Offer it as an experiment. And then offer the people a chance to reflect on the experiment and claim what they have learned.

The results may surprise you.

Then again, they may not.

But the Spirit works by surprise much of the time.

Chapter 10

LAST, JUST DO IT

REMEMBER, HERE ARE THE STEPS for dwelling in the Word:

1. Start with a prayer inviting the Spirit to guide our attending to the Word of God.

2. Turn to Luke 10:1-12, knowing that at some point, you may select your own passage, a story that is related to the story of your group's work. But start with Luke 10: 1-12, because it works for many people all over the world—it is a good starting place. Have Bibles or copies available at every meeting so that the story can be read by different people each time you meet. Set aside without apology at least 20 minutes for this activity.

3. When your group is assembled, begin your meeting with one person reading this passage aloud to the group. Then allow some silence to unfold as people let the words have their impact.

4. Next, instruct folks in this way: Find a person in the group you know least well (we call this person a "reasonably friendly-looking stranger").

Listen that person into free speech as he or she tells you what they heard in the passage. Listen that person into answering one of two questions: 1.)What captured your imagination? or 2.) What question would you like to ask a Biblical scholar?

Listen well, because your job will be to report to the rest of the group what your *partner* has said, not what you yourself said. Some people even take notes to help them focus and remember.

5. Then, turn folks loose with their partners for 6-10 minutes. Notice how *they* are paying attention to one another. When you draw them back together to report what they have heard, ask for them to tell what they learned from their partners.

6. Then wrestle together as a group with what God

might be up to in the passage for your group on that day. Let people know that, as your conversation on other matters continues, anyone at any time may call for the Gospel, and the group will return to the passage.

Final words, but not the last Word

Dwelling in the Word is a habit. It is not a thoughtless, rote habit, although in all human endeavor, habits can become thoughtless and rote. Yet, praise God, the Spirit can work with us even when we are thoughtless and rote. The Spirit uses whatever space we give to create an environment of spiritual discernment. Just when you feel there is nothing more that can be said about Luke 10, someone will say something completely new about Luke 10. That's the thing about habits. They shape us and our behavior. And, like all habits, Dwelling in the Word can be learned and must be chosen.

If you and your group choose Dwelling in the Word, we believe that the Holy Spirit will bless the time you give to it. We have seen such blessings over and over and over again. We read notes from people with whom we've done fairly complex consulting work, notes that say how, again and again, they are struck by what the Spirit accomplishes in them as they practice dwelling in the Word together. We read papers from our students in some very demanding courses, papers that name dwelling in the Word as the activity that focused their group or opened new conversation just when they needed it.

Dwelling in the Word is not *magical*; it isn't a spell that somehow solves all the difficulties in a group.

Not Magical

It is not *formulaic*; if you choose these 12 verses from Luke and read them in the same translation with the same partners every time, you won't finally arrive at the Truth. You will in fact open up many perspectives and interpretations over time, and many voices who are at first quite reluctant may grow strong and brave, saying things they may never have risked saying before. That openness will not make things more single-minded but rather more complex over time, and more rich, helping your group in its discernment to see more possibilities in the Spirit, even as the Spirit helped the people of God to see in the Scriptures and throughout the history of Christianity.

Dwelling is also not *prescriptive*; it doesn't tell you whom to befriend and whom to avoid, what to eat and how to cure, even though we may wish that the scriptures could show us simple answers to the complexities we face. In short, dwelling in the Word cannot solve all of your group's challenges.

But dwelling in the Word, over time, forms a community of the Holy Spirit, where the Spirit is as welcome and expected a presence as any of the human beings in the group. It gives people the chance to be listened into free speech. It gives everyone a more equitable access into the conversation and the community that is being formed in the scriptural story. And, over time, it gives the group the chance to see that they are living a story, and that their story is a part of God's story. It is not magic or formulaic or prescriptive. It is holy. It creates the community of good will that opens time and space for spiritual discernment for the sake of God's mission.

Acknowledgements

WE CALL IT DWELLING IN THE WORD. We have done so since 1995 when Pat Taylor Ellison published a chapter about the habit. But its history and our deep gratitude to many cherished partners go back much farther.

- to a course called Truth and Meaning, taught in the 1980s and early 1990s at Luther Seminary by Donald Juel and Pat Keifert,

- to Pat Taylor Ellison's 1990-1995 dissertation work with 14 congregations from the Southwestern Minnesota Synod of the ELCA and their beautiful reflections on scripture, framed within Ricoeur's "world in front of the text" and their real life struggles to do faithful moral conversation together,

- to Church Innovations Institute's Congregational Studies Research Team that met for four years in the 90s and dwelt in Corinthians and then in Philippians, led in their study by David Fredrickson's profound work,

- to the retreat in 1997 when Mark MacDonald and John Robertson asked for our partnership on their lay catechist project including Gospel-Based Discipleship and in return gave us CI's own dwelling text: Luke 10:1-12,

· and of course way, way back to the foundational practice of *Lectio Divina* and its many forms, some of them even used by Protestants and their leaders, such as Martin Luther.

No book happens without the constant vigilant work of editors like our own Kendra Rosencrans, without creative designers like Peter Gloege, without faithful production teams like Barbara Miller and Caroline Hvidsten, without encouraging advisors like Pat Judd. And this book is even further graced with the drawings of Nico Simpson, our South African friend and genius who can draw a line and a circle together so well that you can tell how that little image is feeling.

To these persons and all those who, through our more than 20 years of work together, taught us by their patience, aptness, and brilliance, we owe our deepest thanks.

Dwelling in the Word

Experience and adopt for your congregation this tested habit for deep listening to God, one another, and your neighbor. Live into a Bible passage and see how it shapes your group's imagination and vision for God's mission through your church. Learn how this habit can make a real difference in your congregation's shared life and work.

START OR JOIN A
DWELLING IN THE WORD
LEARNING COMMUNITY.

TO LEARN MORE VISIT:
WWW.CHURCHINNOVATIONS.ORG

OR CALL:
651-644-3653

Thriving in Change (TIC)

Experience and adopt for your congregation a 20-year tested process for spiritual discernment: deep listening to God, to one another, and to your neighbor. Thriving in Change helps you create time and space in your church for God to be part of your conversation and decision-making, your shared life and mission.

START OR JOIN A
THRIVING IN CHANGE
LEARNING COMMUNITY.

TO LEARN MORE VISIT:
WWW.CHURCHINNOVATIONS.ORG
OR CALL:
651-644-3653

Is your congregation ready to move from DOING mission to being MISSIONAL?